APPALACHIAN
VALUES

A bible and a kerosene lamp
in the home of Godfrey and Bess Issacs,
Floyd's Branch, Jackson County, Kentucky.

APPALACHIAN
VALUES

by
Loyal Jones

Photography by
Warren E. Brunner

With an Introduction by
John B. Stephenson

The Jesse Stuart Foundation
1994

Designed by Jim Marsh

APPALACHIAN VALUES
The Jesse Stuart Foundation

Library of Congress Cataloging-in-Publication Data

Jones, Loyal, 1928-
Appalachian values / by Loyal Jones ; photographs by Warren E. Brunner.
   p. cm.
   ISBN 0-945084-43-9 : $19.95
    1. Appalachian Region, Southern–Civilization–Juvenile literature.
2. Values–Appalachian Region, Southern–Juvenile literature.
3. Appalachian Region, Southern–Social life and customs–Juvenile literature.
4. Appalachian Region, Southern–Pictorial works–Juvenile literature. I. Brunner, Warren E.
II. Title.
F217 .A65J66 1994
974--dc20   94-4372
                                  CIP
                                  AC

First Edition

Published by:
The Jesse Stuart Foundation
P.O. Box 391
Ashland, KY 41114
1994

CONTENTS

Barry Bowles and his mule,
Sand Gap, Kentucky, take a break
from harrowing.

PREFACE

The idea for this book was hatched by Betty Payne James, of Disputanta, Kentucky, then an editor for the Texas Tech Press in Lubbock. I had sent her an essay entitled "Appalachian Values," written earlier to counter the persistent negative stereotypes about Appalachian people by listing and commenting on positive values or characteristics. Betty thought the essay would make a good text for a book of photographs about the people of the region.

So, I approached my old friend Warren Brunner, who has photographed Appalachian people for forty years. He had recently retired, and in cleaning out his studio, he came up with several hundred photographs. After months of sorting and selecting pictures and identifying people, we put the book together. As it turned out, Betty James' idea of doing regional books at the Texas Tech Press did not work out, nor was my regular publisher interested in a picture book.

However, in a telephone conversation, Jim Gifford, Executive Director of the Jesse Stuart Foundation, inquired about my recent work, and I mentioned the manuscript. He immediately showed interest, commenting that the Foundation was thinking of new books that might give Appalachian children a positive view of their Appalachian culture, because of the negative images that many students hold of themselves and the region. So, here is the book.

We thank Betty Payne James for the idea of this book and all of the people who posed for Warren Brunner and whose images appear herein. I want to thank those who have always been generous in helping me to understand the culture and values of the region, beginning with my own kin in Cherokee and Clay Counties in North Carolina. I should note that the stories used to illustrate various values have appeared in the following books put together by Billy Edd Wheeler and myself and published by August House Publisher in Little Rock: *Laughter in Appalachia: A Festival of Southern Mountain Humor* (1987); *Curing the Cross-Eyed Mule: Appalachian Mountain Humor* (1989); and *Hometown Humor, U.S.A.* (1991).

We hope that the reader will feel some of the pleasure that we have had in putting the book together.

Loyal Jones
Berea Kentucky

7

Berea College students
and Professor George Noss
view the sunrise from east pinnacle,
overlooking Big Hill, Kentucky.

INTRODUCTION

Who really knows Appalachia? Why do we torture ourselves with endless, answerless questions: How high? How wide? How distinctive? How deserving? How Elizabethan? How emblematic of America? How representative of the human condition?

It is, I think, because Appalachia is not one thing, and, some would say, perhaps not a thing at all, but a manufactured idea with no counterpart in reality. At the same time, we are not able to leave it alone. It recurs to us over and over again, imposing itself as a guest in our minds, an idea which, like a disobedient dog, will not lie still. Here I am, it says, licking our hands, and I will not go away. Here I am, but who am I?

Many have approached this question, and have backed away in confusion. Some have answered it in bold confidence but with eyes only half-open. Collectors have captured small parts of it and put them on display like pinned butterflies. The press reports mostly the mud and the blood; darkness and night often seem the preferred metaphors, and one wonders whether the sun ever shines in the pines, in the pines.

In Loyal Jones, however, one finds revelation from someone who has lived the mountain life, lived the region, transcended it and come back to interpret it for us in ways that are simply not available to most of us. He is the son of the mountains who has seen the world, thought deeply about it, and returned to consider the place of Appalachia in the universe, a man who once, returning from sea duty in the Navy, said when he saw a mountain, "I loved the sea with its power and beauty, its fury and its tranquility, but how I wanted to see the mountains, and I knew I must go back to them." He has been back in them ever since, serving as master story teller, teacher, guide, and cultural interpreter of the southern mountain region for over forty years.

No single piece of Loyal Jones' writing has deserved and received more attention than his essay, "Appalachian Values," an expanded version of which serves as the text for this book. First published in Twigs in 1973, and reprinted many times since, these ruminations on the soul of a region reveal with sparkling clarity the core elements of regional culture, the bones upon which the flesh of a people is layered.

In this seminal exposition, Loyal Jones is able to see the people of the mountains simultaneously from close and afar; it is as though he had one eye on a microscope and the other at a powerful telescope. It is a wonderful example of the advantage owned exclusively by an observer who is both native and alien, liberated from provincialism but yet anchored firmly in a very particular place. Apart and yet at one with the people, he sees determined individuals, families, and communities attempting to construct decent lives.

It is most important to note the absence of that debilitating quality which so often handicaps observers of Appalachia: the romance with quaintness. Loyal Jones does not claim too much for Appalachian values. Appalachian culture is neither cute nor a snake-oil cure for all of America's problems. Indeed, he goes to some pains to show the limitations and disadvantages of regional values, allowing at one point that they may "keep us from putting either foot forward." Yet, he rightly concludes, "There are many strengths in Appalachian culture...which have been lost in much of America."

Together with Warren Brunner's priceless and dedicated photographic documentation, Loyal Jones' words remind us of the essential qualities of the people of the southern mountains—and indeed of people everywhere—that they will struggle and survive, that they aspire to decency, that they live in the light as well as in the dark.

"All work in Appalachia," Jones concludes, "must be based on the genuine needs as expressed by mountain people themselves. What ever work is done must be done with the recognition that Appalachian culture is real and functioning."

Herchel Logston, Berea, Kentucky,
sniffs sassafras root bark
he has dug for tea.

Who really knows Appalachia? If a monument should be erected in honor of anyone who perfectly and selflessly embodies the complex spirit of the southern mountains, let it be for Loyal Jones. In the meantime, this book is a fitting tribute to his penetrating wisdom and his intense, persistent commitment to the people of the southern mountain region.

John B. Stephenson
President
Berea College
January 25, 1994

*A pioneer cabin
preserved at Fontana Village,
North Carolina.*

1

APPALACHIAN
VALUES

We mountain people are the product of our history and the beliefs and outlook of our foreparents. We are a traditional people, and in our rural setting we valued the things of the past. More than most people, we avoided mainstream life and thus became self-reliant. We sought freedom from entanglements and cherished solitude. All of this was both our strength and our undoing.

Our Appalachian forebears came in almost equal thirds from England, Scotland and Germany, although some came from Wales, France, Holland and Africa. And, of course, the Cherokees were here over a thousand years before Europeans settled.

Mary Belle Bonds,
Orlando, Rockcastle County,
Kentucky.

Green Hubbard,
Horse Lick, Jackson County,
Kentucky.

Jim Jones,
Owsley Fork, Madison County,
Kentucky.

Louise Maney,
in the Big Meat Pottery Shop.
Cherokee, North Carolina.

Recent histories have made much of the Scotch-Irish, that is, Scots who settled the counties of northern Ireland after 1610 and whose descendents sailed in large numbers to the eastern ports, mostly Philadelphia, in the eighteenth century. Many German, English and Welsh people also settled in Pennsylvania, and this conglomeration of peoples overflowed the population reservoirs there and streamed through the Great Valley that separated the Allegheny-Cumberland Plateau on the west from the mighty Blue Ridge on the east, settling the Virginias and the Carolinas and later Tennessee and Kentucky.

Troy Danner, a blacksmith,
sharpens his hatchet on a grindstone
in Valle Crucis, North Carolina.

*Lou Malicote shows pride
in her flowers at her home
in Duff, Tennessee.*

Clarence "Skinny" Rivers,
of Berea, Kentucky,
is a man of convictions.

*A farmer drag-harrows a hillside field
in western North Carolina.*

They came to a land of great natural beauty—high misty mountains, broad valleys and secluded coves and hollows, clear bouncing waters and frothing waterfalls. Wild game, roots and herbs for food and medicine were everywhere. The forests with their towering trees seemed endless, and underneath were rocks and minerals that would attract outsiders later on. For a people escaping from infringements of church and state, Appalachia was ideal for a new way of life, for a time, away from "powers and principalities."

The Pigeon River
in North Carolina.

*The view from Uncle Ben Nicholson's house
in Jackson County, North Carolina.*

Flat Lick Falls,
Jackson County, Kentucky.

Owsley Fork Lake,
near Berea Kentucky,
is peaceful at twilight.

They came for many reasons, but always for new opportunity and freedom—freedom from religious, political, and economic restraints, and freedom to do much as they pleased. The pattern of their settlement shows that they were seeking land and solitude.

Snow covers a hollow
near Disputanta, Kentucky.

Milking time on Mill Creek,
Clay County, Kentucky.

Although many were liter-
ate, evident from their letters,
signing of public documents, and
their possession of books, for a
generation or two they left most
formal schooling behind. This was
a choice of profound significance
for mountain people.

Dudley Snowden reads a favorite poem
to Joyce Ann Hancock in his home
in St. Helen, near Beattyville, Kentucky.

Homer Baker shovels coal
in a Clay County, Kentucky mine.

Eddie Simmons does his homework,
Madison County, Kentucky.

Children, parents and teacher
play a singing game
at Sand Springs School,
Rockcastle County, Kentucky, circa 1965

Life in the wilderness and the continuing relative isolation of Southern mountaineers made a strong imprint on us. The Appalachian value system that influences attitudes and behavior is different in some ways from that held by our modern countrymen, although it is similar to the value system of an earlier America. Following are some of these values.

The Owsley Fork Baptist Church,
Madison County, Kentucky.

2

RELIGION

Mountain people are religious. This does not mean that we always go to church regularly, but we are religious in the sense that most of our values and the meaning we find in life spring from the Bible. To understand mountaineers, one must understand our religion.

In the beginning, they were mostly Anglican, Presbyterian or Baptist, with some Bretheren and Lutherans, all rather formally organized churches with confessions of faith and other creedal documents. Presbyterian and Anglican churches did not serve the spiritual needs of all on the frontier, however, and so locally autonomous groups were formed, depending on local resources and leadership. The Methodists rose

*Converts are baptized
in Red Lick Creek,
Madison County, Kentucky.*

*Elder I. D. Back, moderator
of the Little Dove Old Regular Baptist Church,
preaches before baptizing converts in
Carr Creek, Knott County, Kentucky (Loyal Jones photo).*

*Elders I. D. Back and Ivan Amburgey
baptize Lona Faye Bentley in Carr Creek,
Sassafras, Kentucky*
(Loyal Jones photo)

to prominence in the First Great Awakening of the eighteenth century, stressing the work of the Holy Spirit on human emotions, along with intellectual ideas. The Second Great Awakening, beginning in 1801 in Kentucky, won many Presbyterians and Calvinistic Baptists over to the belief that all who seek the Lord can be saved, not just the limited group that John Calvin said were predestined to be saved. Several churches split over the doctrines of predestination and free-will. Here is a story,

A Free-will Baptist and a Predestinarian Baptist were good friends. One day they went to the courthouse together. As they were coming down stairs from the second floor, the Predestinarian tripped and fell down the stairs, rolling end over end, tearing his suit and bruising himself all over, The Free-Willer rushed down, picked him up, brushed him off and asked how he was.

"Well, I think I'm all right," the man said.

The Free-Willer said, "But I guess you're glad to get that one behind you, aren't you?"

Preacher Martin,
Mill Creek, Clay County,
Kentucky.

Mountain people in large numbers joined the more optimistic Methodist and Free-Will Baptist churches, churches created to an extent by and for the common people. The members depended on the grace of God to help them through a hard world and to save them in the end, even though they at times were weak and sinful. Eventually, other churches grew up in the mountains to meet the needs of isolated people: Cumberland Presbyterians, Disciples of Christ and Churches of Christ, and the Pentecostal-Holiness movement at the turn of the twentieth century added many others, the last group going beyond the Methodists in stressing holiness and the work of grace from the Holy Spirit.

The home mission boards of the mainline denominations have usually looked on our locally autonomous churches as something that we must be saved from. Thus they have sent many missionaries to us, even if we thought we were already secure in the Lord. Many social reformers have also viewed the local church negatively as a hindrance to social progress, since native Christians sometimes have a dim view of human perfectability. What such outside observers fail to see is that our religion has helped to sustain us and has made life meaningful in grim situations. Religion has shaped our lives, but at the same time we have shaped our religion, since religion and culture are always intertwined. Life in the mountains until recently did not allow for an optimistic social gospel. Hard work did not always bring a sure reward, and so perhaps some of mountain religion is more fatalistic than elsewhere. The point is to get religion—get saved—and try to keep the faith and endure, hoping for a sure reward in the hereafter. The beliefs are more realistic than idealistic, because we know what theologian Reinhold Niebuhr pointed out, that we see clearly what we should be and what we should do, and yet we fail consistently; that is the human tragedy. Someone said that man and woman were made at the end of the week when God was tired. The Good News is that even though we fail, God loves us anyway, and if we believe, we will be saved.

Cranks Creek Holiness Church,
Harlan County, Kentucky.

Homecoming Day at Mill Creek,
Clay County, Kentucky.

*A family digs a grave
for a departed relative.*

Woodson Lakes, of Floyd's Branch, Kentucky,
is proud of his sheep and border collie.

3

INDEPENDENCE, SELF-RELIANCE AND PRIDE

Several years ago there came a great snowfall in western North Carolina. The Red Cross came to help people who might be stranded without food or fuel. Two workers heard of an old lady way back in the mountains living alone, and they went to see about her, in a four-wheel drive vehicle. After an arduous trip they finally skidded down into her cove, got out and knocked on the door. When she appeared, one of the men said,

"Howdy, ma'am, we're from the Red Cross," but before he could say anything else, the old lady replied,

"Well, I don't believe I'm a-goin to be able to help you any this year. It's been a right hard winter."

John C. Campbell, in his *The Southern Highlander and His Homeland,* remarked that Americans, Southerners, rural dwellers, and farmers are all independent, and went on to say that since highlanders are all of these things, they have "independence raised to the fourth power." Independence, self-reliance and pride were perhaps the most obvious characteristics of mountain people. Our forebears were independent, else they would not have gone to such trouble and danger to get away from encroachments on their freedom. Independence and self-reliance were traits to be admired on the frontier. People banded together to help one another in communities, but the person who did not or could not look after himself and his family was pitied.

Ronnie Baker,
Redbird, Clay County, Kentucky

William McClure crafts a doughbowl
from buckeye wood on his farm
in Rockcastle County, Kentucky.

The Smith brothers, Ronnie and Donnie,
cut tobacco on their family's farm
on Flat Gap Road near Berea, Kentucky.

Merle Bowman,
Breathitt County, Kentucky.

Myrtle Hisle,
Jackson County, Kentucky.

There is a lesson in the mountaineer's all-out search for freedom and independence. We worked so hard for it that many of us eventually lost it. We withdrew from the doings of the larger society, and in ways it passed us by, although not before it bought up most of natural resources around us. We were hired as "hands to exploit the timber, coal, gas and oil, and when most of it was shipped out, many of us were let go into circumstance beyond our control, some maimed and damaged beyond healing, and some of us consigned to poverty.

Coal miners in Clay County, Kentucky:
Matt Martin, Roy Hollin, co-owner of the mine,
Bailey Perry, and Lee Roy Gross, co-owner.

*Roy Hollin directs the work
of Chester Mayfield and Cecil Grubb
in a mine near Manchester, Kentucky.*

A bulldozer works to expose
the coal seam on a strip mine
in Lee County, Kentucky.

Sawlogs heading for an out-of-state mill,
Harlan County, Kentucky.

But our belief in independence and self-reliance is still strong whether or not we are truly independent. We still value solitude, whether or not we can always find a place to be alone. We also value self-reliance, to do things for ourselves, whether or not it is practical to do so—like make a dress, a chair, build a house, repair an automobile, or play a banjo, fiddle or guitar. We get satisfaction from that, in this age when people hire others to do work they used to do, even to provide entertainment.

Ina Johnson and her mule
press the juice from cane to make sorghum,
Madison County, Kentucky

Albert McKinney, a miller,
lives near Brevard, North Carolina

Berea College student David Hawthorne learns tunes from Callie and Charles Isaacs at Kirby Knob in Jackson County, Kentucky.

Homer Ledford, instrument maker
and musician from Winchester, Kentucky,
does hot licks on one of his mandolins.

Pride is mostly a feeling of not wanting to be beholding to other people. We are inclined to try to do things for ourselves, find our way without asking directions when we are lost on the road, or suffer through when we are in need. We don't like to ask others for help. The value of independence and self-reliance, and our pride, is often stronger than desire or need. Here is another independence joke:

A Baptist preacher was asked to preach in the Presbyterian church. The Presbyterian minister asked,

"Will you wear a robe?"

"Do I have to wear a robe?"

"Well, no, you don't have to wear a robe."

"Well, all right, then" said the Baptist, "I'll wear one."

4

NEIGHBORLINESS AND HOSPITALITY

Our independence is tempered by our basic belief in neighborliness and hospitality. Survival on the frontier sometimes required people to be hospitable, to take people in when night caught them on a journey or keep them indefinitely if their house burned down. Until recent times, neighbors joined to help build houses and barns for those who needed them. No greater compliment could be paid a mountain family than that they were "clever folks," meaning that they were quick to invite you to visit and generous with the food. My father told of eating at one home where the only food was sorghum and corn bread, but the host said graciously, "Just reach and get anything you want."

Those receiving hospitality were expected to reciprocate. In the ballad, "Jesse James," known throughout the mountains, the most damning thing said about "that dirty little coward" Robert Ford who shot Jesse was that,

> He ate of Jesse's bread, and
> he slept in Jesse's bed,
> Yet he laid poor Jesse in
> his grave.

We who were brought up on the value of hospitality will always have the urge to invite those who visit to stay for a meal or to spend the night, even though this is not the custom over much of America now, unless a formal invitation is sent out well in advance.

Scotty Winkler, Carlos Alumbaugh,
and Tracy Jenkins from Estill County, Kentucky,
talk things over.

Carroll Parker, his sister Pat Brunner,
and his wife Kae visit with Uncle Charlie Parker
on his front porch in Jackson County, North Carolina

*John Freeman, a biology teacher,
and his wife Grace have retired
near Brevard, North Carolina.*

48

Susie and John Coffey and their pet raccoon
welcome visitors to their home
near Disputanta, Kentucky.

5

FAMILISM

Appalachian people are family-centered. Mountain people usually feel an obligation to family members and are more truly themselves when within the family circle. Family loyalty runs deep and wide and may extend to grandparents, uncles, aunts, nephews, nieces, cousins and even in-laws. Family members gather when there is sickness, death, or a disaster. Supervisors in northern industries have been perplexed when employees from Appalachia have been absent from jobs to attend funerals of distant relatives. Families often take in relatives for extended periods, or even raise children of kin when there is death or sickness in the family. One of the biggest problems reported by officials in cities to which Appalachians have migrated for work is overcrowding in apartments when relatives are taken in until they get work and places of their own. In James Still's novel, *River of Earth*, relatives are invited in by the father even though there isn't enough food for everyone. The mother in desperation burns the house down and moves her family into the tiny smokehouse to get rid of those whom her husband could not ask to leave. Blood is thick in Appalachia. Two brothers were talking. One said, "You know, I've come to the conclusion that Uncle Luther is an S.O.B." The other said, "Yeah, he is, but he's our'n."

The Rev. J. A. Stafford, pastor of Siloam Methodist Church, Valley View, Kentucky (right), is invited to Sunday dinner at the home of Edgar and Elsie Foster. Also invited are Ronnie Richardson, Eddie Richardson, Anita Carol Casey (back), Robbie Casey, and Mark Casey.

James and Ina Taylor pose with their children,
Judith and Ben, and their Belgian draft horses
on their Rockcastle County, Kentucky, farm.

*Mr. and Mrs. Albert Baldwin make baskets
at Woodscreek Lake, Kentucky.*

Hiram Malicoat, Ethel Heywood,
Annie Bratcher and Lou Malicoat visit in
Duff, Tennessee.

The Appalachian family is subject to the same stresses and strains that affect all American families, and there is alienation, divorce, and abuse here as every-where, but there is a strong attachment and commitment to the extended family in Appalachia that is becoming rare in a land where most of us live someplace other than where we were born.

6

PERSONALISM

One of the main aims in life for Appalachians is to relate well to other persons. We will go to great lengths to keep from offending others, even sometimes appearing to agree with them when in fact we do not. It is more important to get along with one another than it is to push our own views. Mountaineers will sometimes give the appearance of agreeing to meetings that they have no interest in or intention of attending, just because they want to be agreeable. This tendency has led outside organizers to accuse some of us of not being reliable. This personalism is one of the reasons confrontation politics have not always worked in the mountains. We are reluctant to confront and alienate someone, if we can avoid it.

If, however, the issues are important enough, we will push the issue, because there is no lack of courage here. The Widow Ollie Combs, Elder Dan Gibson, and Jink Ray were courageous Kentuckians who physically opposed strip miners operating with mineral deeds on their land. Mrs. Combs was carried off a strip mine site and spent Thanksgiving Day in jail for obstructing the mining operation on her land. Gibson held miners and the law off with a rifle to protect the land of a relative who was serving in Vietnam.

Appalachians are tolerant of personal differences. When respecting the right of other people to be themselves, we expect them to respect our right to be ourselves. Many mountaineers, as far south as Alabama and Georgia were anti-slavery in sentiment and fought for the Union in the Civil War, and although Reconstruction legislatures imposed anti-Negro laws, thus training us in segregation, Appalachians, for the most part, have not been saddled with the same prejudices against black people that other Southerners have. We have prejudices, but usually we have not made a crusading cause of them. I know of a Regular Baptist church in eastern Kentucky that has had a integrated membership of working-class people since it was organized in 1911. Another Baptist church, in an adjacent county, was founded by ex-slaves and also has white members. My great-grandparents took in a black orphan in North Carolina in post-Civil War times, and all of the children slept in the same bed. Appalachians fought the Cherokees, and then intermarried with them and generally accepted them as neighbors. This contrasts with attitudes in other parts of the country. We may not always like or approve of other people, but we normally accept them as persons and treat them with respect.

Hettie Powell and Jane Darnell
share stories in Transylvania County, North Carolina

Dr. Jon Strauss of Berea
makes a home visit to Ethel Harrison
at Big Hill, Kentucky.

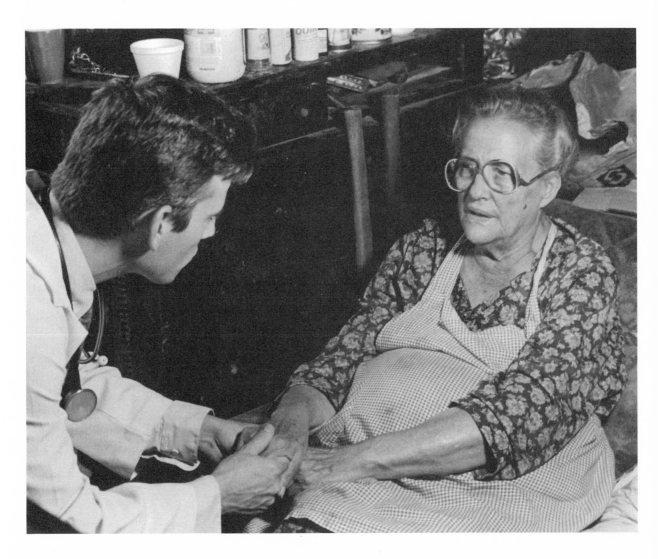

Earl Lee Hysinger (far right)
tries to trade knives with Bill Doan,
while Oscar McClure and Cossie Sowder
look on in Mt. Vernon, Kentucky.

Joyce Parker and her son Jim
do some front porch sitting
on Wolf Mountain, Jackson County,
North Carolina.

We usually relate on a personal basis rather than on how people dress or the credentials or accomplishments they claim. Likewise we think about personalities more readily than abstractions. Jeff Daniel Marion, a Tennessee poet captures this quality in his poem, "In a Southerly Direction," about giving directions to a traveller.

It's Just
over the knob
there—
you know the place,
the one
up there next to
Beulah Justice,
your mother's second cousin
on her daddy's side.
Or
if you go in by
the back road
it's the farm across the way
from Jesse's old barn
that burned down
last June
with them 2 fine mules
of his,
Why hell, son,
you can't miss it.

(Used by permission from Jeff Daniel Marion, <u>Out in the Country Back Home</u>, *Winston-Salem: Jackpine Press, 1976, p. 13.)*

The late Joe Creason, who wrote for the *Louisville Courier-Journal*, told of interviewing a man in Pike County, the eastern-most Kentucky county. After a while, the man said, "Where are you from?" Creason replied, "Louisville." The man reflected for a moment and asked, "Who's the barber over there now?"

We think in terms of persons, we remember the people with whom we are familiar, and we have less interest in abstractions and people that we have only heard about.

7

HUMILITY OR MODESTY

Mountain people value modesty in terms of one's personal attributes or accomplishments. Compliments are deferred with such as, "Well, I really didn't do too well. If I had just had time to practice..." Some even have trouble accepting compliments for their children, and will say something like, "Well, I guess he does pretty well for what he's got to work with." An old lady was asked if she had seen Halley's Comet in 1910, and she replied, "Well, only from a distance."

This modesty is taught. I answered the phone once, and a voice inquired, "Whozis?" Having been to school, I countered, "With whom did you wish to speak?"

There was a long pause, and then the voice came back, "Well, I can tell ye right now by the way you're a-talkin' it's not who I's a-wantin'." I should have learned a lesson, but I didn't. A few weeks later another person on the phone asked, "Who is this?" and I said "With whom did you wish to speak?" The answer was, "You, you stuffy bastard!" It was Jack Weaver, a college classmate who hails from my part of the mountains.

We mountaineers are levellers, and we believe we are as good as anybody else, but no better. We believe that we should not put on airs, not boast, nor try to get above our raising. We usually do not extoll our own virtues, and if we do we are ridiculed by others in subtle ways. Persons who are really accomplished, such as in playing music or singing, are often reluctant to perform until it is determined that you really want to hear them, and then they will preface the performance with disparaging words about their voices or their instruments, "Well, I'll try one but I've had this old cold for a week and don't hardly have any voice left, and I can't keep this old banjer in tune a-tall." The mountain preacher will often talk of his unworthiness for the task at hand and hint that there are others attending who could do a better job, but then will say something like, "But with the help of the Lord, I'll try." Of course, when these formalities are dispensed with, the preacher or musician will probably cut loose with a great deal of vigor and skill.

Albert Baldwin shows off his peach crop
at Woodscreek Lake, Kentucky.

Bruce Greene, of Celo, North Carolina,
John Hermann of Asheville, and Clyde Davenport
of Monticello, Kentucky, get together
for some old-time tunes.

*A girl observes shyly from her doorway
in east Tennessee.*

60

Earl Thomas plays the fiddle
for his mother, Mary Thomas,
near Disputanta, Kentucky.

Donald Harris shows off his puppy
in Richmond, Kentucky.

Josephine Whitaker, member of the
Hound Dog Hookers, works on a rug
in Blackey, Kentucky.

My feeling is that we mountain people have a pretty realistic view of ourselves, and we don't take ourselves too seriously. We temper everything with humor that reflects the human condition as we see it. Since we never think that we can be perfect, we don't become cynical when we fail. When we do not fail, we are pleasantly surprised. These beliefs make us somewhat at peace with ourselves. We don't pretend to be what we are not.

63

A swinging bridge over Red Bird River,
near Oneida, Kentucky.

8

L O V E

O F

P L A C E

One of the first questions asked in the mountains, after "whose boy/girl are you?" is "Where are you from?" We are oriented around place. We remember our homeplace and many of us go back as often as possible. Some of us think about going back for good, perhaps to the Nolichucky, Big Sandy, Hiwassee, or Oconoluftee, or to Drip Rock, Hanging Dog, Shooting Creek, Decoy, Stinking Creek, Sweetwater, or Sandy Mush. Our place is close on our minds. One fellow said he came from so far back in the mountains, the sun set between his house and the road. Our songs tell of our regard for the land where we were born. Sense of place is one of the unifying values of mountain people, and it makes it hard for us to leave the mountains, and when we do, we long to return.

This fellow died and went to heaven. St. Peter showed him around, and he thought everything was up to expectations–streets of gold, heavenly choirs, harps–and then he heard these people in the corner of heaven raising an awful commotion, quarreling, complaining, and shouting. He went over to investigate and found they were all chained to the wall. He said to St. Peter, "Who are these people?"
"They are Appalachian mountaineers, "St. Peter said.
"Why are they chained to the wall?"
St. Peter said, "If we didn't do that they'd go home every week-end."

An eastern Kentucky farmstead.

*Haystacks on a farm
near Loboville, Tennessee.*

A girl walks a lonely road
on Long Branch, Estill County,
Kentucky.

Albert Stewart, an eastern
Kentucky poet reflects a strong
sense of place in his poetry, as
in this one, "Near in Mountains,"
about his parents:

Near, in mountains my youth well knows
And under that self-same star
My mother was born on Troublesome Creek,
My father was born on Carr.

My father rode there to Troublesome Creek
And kissed her beneath that star;
Then Mother came here to live with us—
Here, on the waters of Carr.

Fast flow the waters of Troublesome Creek,
And strong flow the waters of Carr
That never shall bide by the resting place
Where Father and Mother are.

Oh, near is the land where my father lived,
And Troublesome was never so far;
But far and lost my parents lie
High on the ridges of Carr

(Reprinted by permission from Albert Stewart, <u>The Untoward Hills</u>.
Morehead, Kentucky: Morehead State College Press,
1962; rpt. 1987, P. 11.)

James Still, a northern
Alabama native now living in
Hindman, Kentucky, expressed a
feeling of home as well as it has
been said, in a poem entitled
"Heritage."

I shall not leave these prisoning hills
Though they topple their barren heads to level earth
And the forests slide uprooted out of the sky.
Though the waters of Troublesome, of Trace Fork,
Of Sand Lick rise in a single body to glean the valley,
To drown lush pennyroyal, to unravel rail fences;
Though the sun-ball breaks the ridges into dust
And burns its strength into the blistered rock
I cannot leave. I cannot go away.

Being of these hills, being one with the fox
Stealing into the shadows, one with the new-born foal,
The lumbering ox drawing green beech logs to mill,
One with the destined feet of man climbing and descending,
And one with death rising to bloom again, I cannot go.
Being of these hills I cannot pass beyond.

(Used by permission from James Still, The Wolfpen Poems.
Berea, Kentucky: The Berea College Press, 1986, p. 82.)

*Mr. and Mrs. Oscar Carter sit in their general store
in Pulaski County, Kentucky,
among life's necessities and niceties,
including folk art.*

*Campaign signs
on a roadside building
near Duff, Tennessee.*

9

PATRIOTISM

Appalachians have a special feeling about the flag of the United States. This is the land that gave them freedom to be themselves, and when that freedom was threatened, they led in seeking independence. The Fincastle Declaration and the reputed Mecklinburg Declaration were expressions of independence that preceded Jefferson's Declaration of Independence. It was the "overmountain men' who defeated a British army at King's Mountain. Many areas of the mountains were settled by Revolutionary War veterans who were given land in lieu of money for their service. Because of strong feelings for the Union, as well as an aversion to slavery, mountaineers over large areas of

the region supported the Union during the Civil War. West Virginia seceded from Virginia and became a Union state. Kentucky never seceded but was split, and many of the mountain counties had Northern sympathies. East Tennessee was a hotbed of Union sympathizers, and one out of three North Carolinians who fought in the war, fought for the Union. Both Georgia and Alabama had pro-union counties. Winston County, Alabama even seceded from Alabama.

*War on Poverty officials
and local politicians visit a home
in Richmond, Kentucky, in the 1960s.*

Mountaineers have been in all the national wars. Tennessee is known as "The Volunteer State" because of the number of its sons in the War of 1812. The Battle of New Orleans in 1815 spawned a popular song, "The Hunters of Kentucky," who helped carry the battle. In World War I, two Appalachian soldiers stand out, both awarded the Congressional Medal of Honor: Sergeant Alvin York, an east Tennessean, who alone encountered a German infantry company, killing 25 men with as many shots, and capturing 128 enlisted men, four officers and 25 machine guns; and Sergeant Willie Sandlin, an eastern Kentuckian, who with rifle and grenades assaulted and wiped out three machine gun nests to open a hole in the enemy's defense line.

James Jones, in his trilogy of World War II, beginning with *From Here to Eternity*, cast an Appalachian soldier as his "soldier's soldier" in each book, basing him on Letcher County, Kentucky, soldier Robert Stewart, who was in Jones' rifle company. Appalachian military daring extended into the Korean and Vietnam conflicts. Steven Giles, Charles Walter, and Bert Allen, working for the Veteran's Administration, report that in Korea and Vietnam, Appalachian soldiers were killed at a higher rate and won a higher percentage of Medals of Honor than other Americans. For example, in Vietnam the national average for battle deaths was 58.9 for every 100,000 males in the 1970 Census, but for West Virginia it was 84.1. Of all soldiers in the Korean War, 9 percent came from Appalachia; 8 percent were from the region in Vietnam. Yet Appalachians won 18 percent of the Medals of Honor in Korea and 13 percent in Vietnam. Officers told Giles that they would "choose Appalachians for point men and for patrols because they felt they were more motivated, more likely to be woods-wise and more familiar with the use of weapons."

(From an Associated Press story by Leanne Waxman, "Vietnam's cost was high for Appalachian Soldiers: Death toll blamed on 'Sgt. York syndrome.'" <u>Louisville Courier-Journal</u>, *March 15, 1989, p.B1.)*

James Still, Hindman, Kentucky,
poet, short story writer and novelist,
was a sergeant in the Army Air Force in North Africa
during World War II.

Ed Reid, of Berea, Kentucky (left),
poses with an Army buddy
in Korea.

Many Appalachians have became well-known as politicians and regional and national leaders in state offices, the U.S. Senate and House of Representatives and in the Courts.

Tenna Partin, of Frakes, Kentucky,
weaves place mats.

10

SENSE

OF

BEAUTY

We mountaineers have many avenues for artistic expression. Most of the things we made in the past were tied to functional necessities. Great pride was taken in the handicrafts—in the beauty of the wood in a chair, the inlay and carving on a rifle, the stitchery, design and variety of color in a quilt or a vegetable-dyed coverlet. There was also fine craftsmanship in the items that were beyond functional necessities, such as fiddles, banjos, and dulcimers that were played with skill. Appalachian people have created or perpetuated some of the most beautiful songs in folk music, have preserved the great British ballads and made new ones based on local tragedies. Numerous Appalachians have made a name for themselves in folk and country music. We have re-told the Old World tales about Jack and giants, witches and dragons and made up new tales. We have also been masters of the simile and metaphor sometimes in archaic language, such as "He'd cross hell on a rotten rail to get a drink of liquor," or "She's cold as a kraut crock," or "He looks like the hind wheels of hard times." These are statements that involve the imagination.

Charles Horrar,
blacksmith of Berea, Kentucky,
makes the sparks fly.

Chester Cornett,
of Knott County, Kentucky,
demonstrates chairmaking.

Glenna Angel and Joyce Ward
put the finishing touches on a quilt
at Crazy Quilt Crafts in Newcomb, Tennessee.

Virgil Crowe makes Cherokee tribal masks
in Cherokee, North Carolina.

Carmen Scott plays the guitar
beside a log building
on the Berea College campus.

Smith Ross, Pine Knot, Kentucky,
demonstrates a gee-haw a Whimmy-diddle
at a crafts fair in Berea.

Spurgeon Holland
enjoys a laugh in Brevard,
North Carolina.

11

SENSE OF HUMOR

We have a good sense of humor, although it is sometimes delivered in a deadpan fashion, in keeping with our sense of modesty and understatement. Humor is more than fun; it is a coping mechanism in sickness or hard times. We tend to poke fun at ourselves, saying self-deprecating things like, "I was hiding behind the door when the looks were passed out." Our humor is tied up with our concept of the human condition. We see humor when people make pretensions to power and perfection and inevitably fail. We may poke fun at pompous people, or try to "get their goat" by playing practical jokes on them. We may say, for example, of those who aspire to learning, "Preachers and lawyers and buzzard's eggs, there's more hatched than come to perfection."

Sonja Dudley,
Madison County, Kentucky,
shows that appreciation of humor starts early.

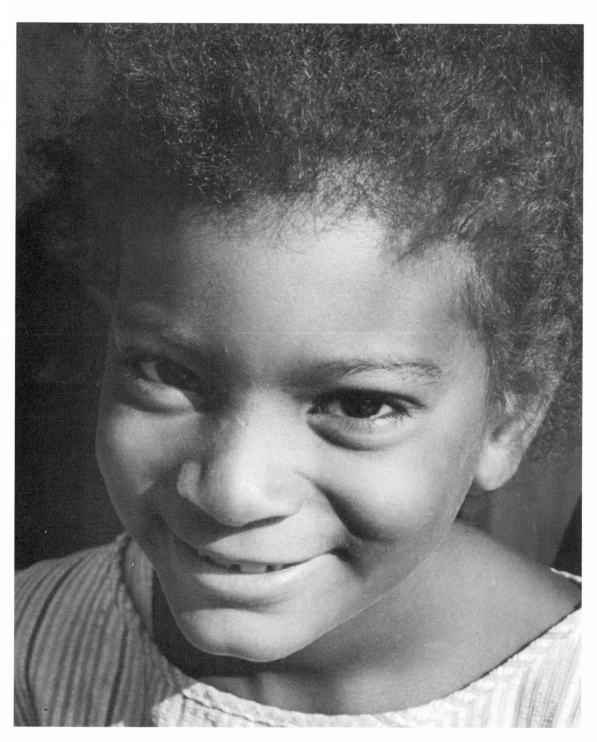

Billy Wilson had many stories to tell
in his shoe shop in Berea, Kentucky,
before retiring to full-time fishing.

Susan Deaton and daughter Carolyn Deaton
get a laugh out of a big potato
in their garden in Barwick, Kentucky.

Miley Cain, of Berea, Kentucky,
gets into humorous situations
in his gravel business

John Coffey,
of Disputanta, Kentucky,
gets off a good one.

Sometimes the humor reflects hard times, like when the woman went to ask the governor to pardon her husband who was in the penitentiary,

"What's he in for?" the governor asked.
"For stealing a ham."
"Well, that doesn't seem too serious," the governor said. "Is he a good man?"
"No, he's a mean old man."
"Is he a hard worker?"
"No, he won't hardly work a-tall.
"Well, why would you want a man like that out of prison?"
"Well, Governor, I'll be honest with you. We're out of ham."

I once told stories like this to a group of missionaries in Appalachia to illustrate a speech. Afterwards a grim-looking couple came up and asked where I had learned such stories. I said that they came from mountain people. They said they didn't believe it. I asked why, and they said, "We don't believe people with that many problems would have a sense of humor and tell such stories." I said, "We do have problems, and perhaps humor is one way that we can cope." Being modest, I didn't tell them that they had a lot to learn about mountain people and that they needed to develop a little bit of a sense of humor if they expected to work in the mountains.

Early morning light on Red Lick,
Estill County, Kentucky.

*Morning on Roan Mountain
in Tennessee.*

The view from Burnt Bridge Road,
Rockcastle County, Kentucky.

Red Lick Road,
Madison County, Kentucky.

A snowy pasture
near Berea, Kentucky.

I have written of the values which I think are good, that I take pride in knowing are held by my people. Some of these beliefs, however, can be a disadvantage to us, sometimes keeping us from putting our best foot, or either foot, forward. Our "fatalistic" religious attitudes may cause us to take a "what will be will be" attitude toward social problems and public responsibility. Our Calvinistic attitude toward the human condition sometimes inhibits us from trying to change the nature and behavior of people. Our independence often keeps us from getting involved, from creating a sense of community, cooperation, and devotion to social causes. Our attachment to place may keep us from venturing forth to improve ourselves and our situations. We are so involved with persons that we have not taken proper notice of ideas and organizations which are necessary in today's society. We have been hospitable and neighborly to strangers, who have at times deceived us. We have been modest and unassertive, and thus have let others from elsewhere do jobs that we ought to have done ourselves, and then have found that they were not done the way we wanted anyhow. Finally we have been so close to the frontier with its exploitive mentality, that we have seen our natural resources and our environment squandered for profit, and we have seen our neighbors exploited too and have

*Wintry afternoon
on Burnt Bridge Road,
Rockcastle County, Kentucky.*

Boys take a swim
in Greasy Creek, Leslie County, Kentucky,
on a hot summer day.

not taken concerted action against these threats. Our sense of freedom has often bordered on license, and we have thrown our trash over the mountains and into streams to add to mining and industrial pollution. In our modest way, we have watched, and looked the other way, and our problems have closed in on us. We know now that we have to take responsibility for our actions, and jointly with our neighbors, make sure that others take responsibility also. We are acting responsibly by creating and joining organizations throughout the region that are calling on private and public interests to clean up their acts and lobbying legislatures to pass laws that will correct abuses and make the region a better place to live.

But there are strengths in Appalachian culture, strengths that have been lost or weakened in mainstream American culture. Strengthening qualities must be preserved and nurtured, as we attempt to change the qualities that diminish the chance for a better life. Social and economic plans for Appalachia must be based on needs outlined by the mountain people themselves. Whatever work that is done must be done with the recognition that Appalachian culture is real and functioning. This implies that change may not come easily and will not come at all unless the reasons for change are sound and are desired by mountain people.

Onions drying
in Jackson County, Kentucky.

*A mother cares for her children
in Rockcastle County, Kentucky.*

WARREN BRUNNER

Warren Brunner is a fixture in Berea. Years ago, when you came to town you might see him ambling along the street with a camera swung around his neck or a tripod on his shoulder. With him was a photographic subject dressed to the nines. They were heading toward the Berea College Appalachian Museum with its log cabin and rail fence, background for many of Brunner's special pictures. He knows how to make almost everybody look good in a portrait. He thinks he has done over a thousand weddings in the four decades he has been in Berea, and hundreds of proms, dances, and other events. But Warren isn't doing much commercial photography any more, since he turned his shop over to his daughters. Now he's doing what he used to do only in his spare time–photographing people and scenes in Appalachia.

If you drive out in the country around Berea, you may see Warren's van parked alongside the road and Warren nowhere in sight. He's probably hiking up an unexplored road or across the mountain to visit a potential subject. Sometimes, he hitch-hikes out of town, hoping for a ride with somebody interesting who might just invite him home for a visit and a few pictures. Or he may drive a county or two from Berea and then hike the backroads. His wife Pat, a photographer herself, expects him home when she sees him coming. Warren often goes on long camping trips in the mountains, sometimes with family or friends, but often alone. He can make friends with anybody. Soon he is taking pictures of his new friends, their children, dogs, mules, cows, or whatever, and if he sees an interesting view or a building, he photographs those too. Over the years he has been generous in making copies of such pictures for his subjects. Others have wound up on living room walls, bought by visitors to Brunner Studio or to the annual fairs of the Kentucky Guild of Artists and Craftsmen, of which he is a member.

He has interesting stories to tell about his jaunts. He once found a 96-year-old bachelor and asked him to pose for him. Dressed up in hat, suit, and tie, the man made an impressive picture. When Warren went back to visit him again, his elderly sisters said that he wasn't home and allowed, "He's out gallivanting."

Warren grew up in Bayfield and Eau Claire, Wisconsin, and when his father gave him a camera at the age of 14, he began taking pictures, hundreds of them, of children, boats and harbor scenes. He became the high school annual staff photographer, and he eventually got a job as photographer for the *Eau Claire Leader-Telegram*. He continued taking pictures during two years in the Navy. After an apprenticeship in Fond Du Lac, he answered an advertisement and became manager of the Mattson Studio in Berea, Kentucky. In 1960, he bought the studio. He mostly did portraits and weddings, but occasionally he slipped off and photographed in the mountains. Warren says this of Appalachian photography:

As I think of my photographic experiences in Appalachia, I received my introduction to the mountains and their people during "The War on Poverty." Photographers were called upon to show the needs of the people, and some did it with more sensitivity than others.

Although this statement implies that his interest was commercial, he took many pictures of conditions on his own, and in recent years he has re-photographed some of the same people and places from the 1960s at his own expense. Recently he said:

Now I'm retracing my steps, to take a second look at the land and people. I want to help others through calendars and books, slide shows, and working with non-profit organizations to portray the needs of the land and people.

*A student stokes the coal stove
in a 1960s one-room school
in Jackson County, Kentucky.*

He has been busy in this new phase of his career. He has done two books with Al Fritsh, S. J., who works with Appalachia-Science in the Public Interest. He has produced calendars for the past decade or so, depicting mountain life. He has also done slide shows, one in cooperation with four social workers to show the strengths of mountain people and to combat negative stereotypes, and another in cooperation with Berea College sociology professor Thomas Boyd to document one of the first poverty programs in eastern Kentucky. Warren has also taken 3000 photographs of mountain churches to illustrate forthcoming

*Heading down Interstate 75
near Berea, Kentucky.*

books by Dr. Deborah McCauley. He is making prints of pictures he made over the past 30 years which will be available to other writers and publishers.

He is still roaming the hills, on his own, or for non-profit agencies. The transition from commercial photographer (to make people look handsome, pretty or at least respectable) to documentary photographer (to present Appalachia as it is) appears complete. Warren likes the idea of documenting life, but he usually describes his work as "mountain pictorials." James Still, the noted Kentucky writer, described Brunner's work succinctly in an inscription in one of his books, "For Warren Brunner, who helped Appalachia see and remember itself."

Loyal Jones